I0487857

CYBER AWARE

The Code

J.E. Franks-Belgrave

The United States of America
Commonwealth of Virginia
City of Hampton
Cyberspace
--Self- Published--

First Printing: 2019

ISBN 978-0-359-65457-4

Self Published. Year of our Lord 2019

PO Box 7170
Hampton, Virginia 23666
https://www.cnvta.club

Ordering Information:

Special discounts are available on quantity purchases by corporations, associations, educators, and others. For details, contact the publisher at the above listed address
or e-mail the publisher at cybernotaryvta@gmail.co

About the Cover of the book: designed by the author of this book.

CONTENTS

ABOUT THE AUTHOR

President of NotaryNow LLC. Head of the first Cyber Notary Virtual Training Academy in the Commonwealth of Virginia, USA. Airman at the United States Air Force Reserve. Also served with the Kentucky Air National Guard. Advocate of Cyber Awareness and the use of Digital tools that empower Small Businesses. Have her small business participating as Champion in Cyber Awareness Programs such as the one led by *The National Cyber Security Alliance.*

Author of Remote/Webcam Notarization: Basic Understanding; Cyber Education Series; Notary Public Essentials; Cyber Liability Insurance; Commissioning as Notary Public and Notary Signing Agent after 40.

Mother of two beautiful Beagles. Wife of a professional, fun, supportive husband.

One of the Author's sayings:

"Be Safe. Have Fun. Make it Count."

PREFACE

Nine years ago, I wrote an article titled "Cyber-Awareness in the New Year." The article was published by a local military newspaper. It was clear that, back then, my target audience was the airmen and their families in our United States Air Force. Years have passed and the necessity for cyber-awareness has increased. As technology continues to advance and devices connected to a Grid[1] become more accessible to the general public, the cyberworld's security faces more vulnerabilities. The truth is: the more educated you become in cyberspace affairs, cyber-reality hits your fingers, your voice, your eyes, and any means in which you enter, navigate, and conduct yourself in and out of the internet.

Despite vulnerabilities, feel confident about utilizing digital tools available in Cyberspace. The Code to a safer cyberenvironment will be your first weapon of defense in a world where ones and zeros, highs and lows, true and false play roles in communication, creation, execution, and cyber deployments.

If you are a Cyber Notary, enjoy this book and continue your Cyber Education. Sign up and get certified as Online Notarization Specialist at the *Cyber Notary Virtual Training Academy* (CNVTA) https://www.cnvta.club

---

[1] Grid: in computing, it is the use of widely distributed computer resources to reach a common goal.

CHAPTER 1

INTRODUCTION TO CYBERSPACE

As amazing as it might seem, "Cyberspace", a widely used term by technology industry leaders, entered our culture via Science Fiction and the Arts[2]. The term Cyberspace usually references to a Global perspective of life and transactions via the internet.

When trying to understand the word "Cyberspace", think of a virtual space without boundaries. Cyberspace is where virtual reality[3] takes place. Nowadays, most people link virtual reality with computer gaming; however, there is much more going on in a virtual space than just playing games.

The word Cyberspace is a fusion of Cyber and Space. Anything "Cyber" refers to anything dealing within the global system of interconnected computer networks that follows the structure of an already established protocol in order to link devices together worldwide.

For the reader who is just beginning to understand how the internet works, picture the following: the moment you allow your computer to connect to the internet, your computer's unique address, known as IP, begins to navigate the journey you set your

---

[2] The term "Cyberspace" was first used by the American-Canadian author William Gibson in 1982 in a story published in Omni magazine and then in his book *Neuromancer*.

[3] Virtual Reality: created by computer software; visual but intangible.

computer to take. Once you allow your device to have access to the internet, your device communicates with other devices that are already linked to the particular destination you commanded your device to get to. IP means Internet Protocol. If your device has access to the internet, then, your device already understands the language of the internet and communicates via its unique IP. Remember, you are the user, the commander. Your device is like a lamp with a Ginni inside. It will only do what you command it to do.

Your device is also your portal to Cyberspace. Many people have invested thousands of hours in navigating and building up anything and everything found in Cyberspace to the extent of visualizing Cyberspace as a Global City. Who knows, maybe in the future Users will be considered global citizens of Cyberspace. The point is: Cyberspace has evolved so much that it has its dark side as well.

One of the dark sides of Cyberspace is known as the Dark Web[4]. As a safe User, you do not want to put your cybernavigation at risk by entering the Dark Web. Everything you need or might be looking for on the internet might be accessible in legal and safer ways. Some people are curious and they put together the tools needed to navigate the Dark Web. For what I found in my research about the Dark Web, I do not recommend Users to fall for it.

Besides the Dark Web, there is something known as Dark Internet. The Dark Internet and the Dark Web are not the same.

---

[4] Dark Web: found within the Deep web. The black sheep of the Dark Internet.

Dark Web, Deep Web, and Dark Internet

Maybe one of the characteristics that make the Dark Web, Deep Web, and the Dark Internet similar to each other is the fact that their content cannot be searched in known search engines such as Google, Bing, Firefox, etc; by just typing words. These three interesting cyberspaces require special cybertools or special browsers to explore them.

DARK WEB	DEEP WEB	DARK INTERNET
▪It is said that it is mostly used for illegal activities.	-The entire web that is not accessible by conventional search engines. **(The Dark web is within the Deep Web)** The Deep web is much larger than the Dark Web.	-Mostly for legal activities such as storing scientific research only a few are interested in.

Internet activities are trackable, why would users risk their presence on the internet by engaging in illegal activities?

Like in the real/tangible world where some people engage in illicit activities, the same happens over the internet.

It turns out that there are special cybertools that camouflage IP addresses on the internet or makes it difficult to figure which IP address is doing what (Remember, your computer or the computer you use has a unique IP address already assigned. It is the IP address that communicates all over the internet). Whenever Users are on the Surface; visible web, IP addresses are easier to trace. However, there is no need to worry because, on the Surface, most people are doing legal business, transactions, navigation, or the normal expected on the expected human being surfing the web. If you are not doing anything wrong or illegal, no need to worry. (Remember to ignore links you do not know about or those links that look suspicious to you).

Why is this information important or relevant?

Imagine visiting a new city where you just want to conduct business or have a safe vacation. After you are done, you just want to return home safe and without worries lingering in your mind. It is the same every time you navigate the internet for whichever purpose you were on Cyberspace.

When you are online, another way to remember where you are at is by looking at the graphic on the next page.

Graphic 1

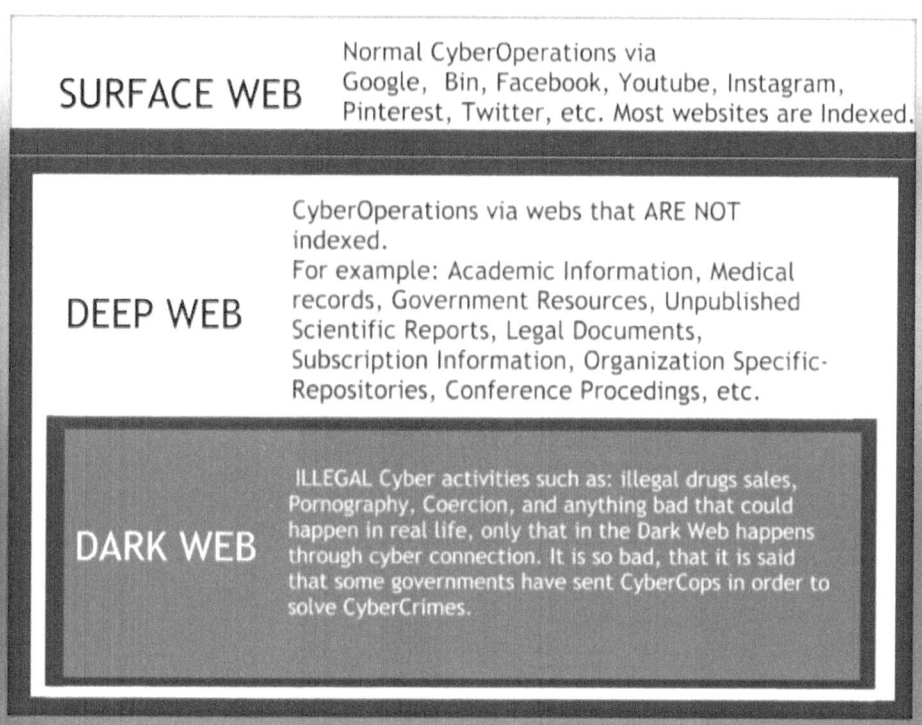

SURFACE WEB	Normal CyberOperations via Google, Bin, Facebook, Youtube, Instagram, Pinterest, Twitter, etc. Most websites are Indexed.
DEEP WEB	CyberOperations via webs that ARE NOT indexed. For example: Academic Information, Medical records, Government Resources, Unpublished Scientific Reports, Legal Documents, Subscription Information, Organization Specific-Repositories, Conference Procedings, etc.
DARK WEB	ILLEGAL Cyber activities such as: illegal drugs sales, Pornography, Coercion, and anything bad that could happen in real life, only that in the Dark Web happens through cyber connection. It is so bad, that it is said that some governments have sent CyberCops in order to solve CyberCrimes.

Keep your Cyber-awareness active at all times when navigating Cyberspace.

CH 1 REVIEW

➤The term Cyberspace usually references to a Global perspective of life and transactions via the internet.

➤The word Cyberspace is a fusion of Cyber and Space.

➤The Dark Web is not the same as the Dark Internet.

➤The Dark Web lives within the Deep Web.

➤The Dark Internet is more than just the Dark Web.

➤Web = "World Wide Web" and it is only a % of the Internet.

➤The Deep Web cannot be indexed; therefore, it is considered hidden internet.

Stay on the Cyberspace mindset and continue to the next chapter.

THE CODE TO A SAFER CYBER-ENVIRONMENT

How can anyone be safe in the current cyber-environment where many minds from all traits have access to Cyberspace? The answer is not focused on those minds, but in you, your mind, and your user habits.

In order to understand the code, you must first develop qualities of a **cautious user**. These qualities are learned and practiced until they become natural in you.

What are the qualities of a cautious user?

A cautious user is someone navigating cyberspace, intentionally, avoiding potential problems. For example, a user capable of overcoming impulsiveness and unnecessary curiosity when navigating the internet can be considered a cautious user. As a cautious user know your purpose of the visit to Cyberspace before entering cyberspace. Know the purpose and stay on course. Deviation from the purpose might lead you to unnecessary exposure.

In the previous Chapter, I mentioned an area of Cyberspace that users are better off away from; the Dark Web. Remember, the Dark Web will not appear in front of the eyes of the user unless the user is using special navigating tools that allow access to the Dark Web. In the most known surface of the Web, links or pop-ups from unwanted organizations may show up. Also, links that may trigger the curiosity of the user may show up as an advertisement. A cautious user does not click on the links that have nothing to do with the purpose of the visit to Cyberspace.

Software Maintenance

Keeping updated the software your computer runs in order to access the internet is another highly important step to take and repeat as many times as needed. Running outdated applications while navigating the internet might put your computer and peripherals connected to your computer at risk of being impacted by malware deployed by malicious entities present in cyberspace. Unfortunately, Cyberspace has become a space where the good, the bad, and the ugly also play roles for committed reasons or just as games some people play in order to expose the vulnerabilities available. Where there is a vulnerability, most likely, there will be a hacker trying to exploit it. You, as the user, want to counter anything that could make your cyber-navigation vulnerable. The great maintenance of the software your computer uses is one step to counter unhealthy intentions freely floating on Cyberspace and waiting for that open door or open vulnerability to crawl in.

As you may know by now, many electronic devices have the capacity to connect via blue-tooth and wi-fi (IEEE 802.11).

INTERNET CONNECTIVITY

Wired connectivity and Wireless connectivity.

Will try my best to explain this as easy as possible.

Wired Connectivity:

If you have heard of DSL connectivity, then, you may have an idea what wired internet connectivity is. If not, here it is: **DSL** is a wired transmission that uses traditional copper telephone lines already installed to homes and businesses. A modem in your home connects the computer or wireless router to a copper telephone line using an Ethernet cable. An advantage of DSL service is that it works with existing wiring. The phone line connects to a digital subscriber line. The rest of the connection is taken care of by the telephone central office. The only equipment needed is a modem plugged into an existing phone jack and filters for each telephone in your home or office. This type of connection depends on the distance between your home or office and the service provider. Upload and downloads speeds may vary as well. Developing technologies may make DSL services obsolete. However, if your home or office has access to **fiber optics**, a technology that converts electrical signals to light pulses (on/off) and sends the light pulses through transparent glass fibers about the diameter of a human hair, your internet connectivity might be on a better position. Technology via Fiber Optics is faster than DSL and there is less signal degradation as well.

How to secure your Wired Connectivity

According to globussoft.com, there are 5 essential steps to secure your wired network.

1-Auditing and Mapping:
This step consists of understanding the network infrastructure, network location, vendor model, and basic configurations of firewalls.

2-Network update:
Check for firmware and software updates. Also, check if default passwords have been changed or not.

3-MAC Address filtering:
It is a security method based on access control. MAC address filtering adds an extra layer of security that checks the device's MAC address against a list of agreed addresses. If the client's address matches one on the router's list, access is granted otherwise it doesn't join the network. This will give you more control over the different devices which are connected to the network.

4- Use Virtual Private Networks (VPN):
This type of network is used to create a secure network connection over the public network or the private network on the Internet. In this step, you are able to secure your network with unique IDs and Passwords and also encrypt your server and all your traffic.

5- Physically, secure the Network:

At work, make sure only assigned people have access to the equipment, servers, and cables connected to the wired network. Ensure you have a plan to protect your wired network from outsiders. If necessary, use locked cabinets and locked doors. Protect your wired Network in every way possible.

Protect you Wired Network.

Protect it from "Outsiders".

Wireless Connectivity:

This is the type of connection that does not require a cable in order to transmit or receive communication. This is the type of computer network that does not require cables in order to establish a connection. Wireless connectivity functions via radio waves and/or microwaves in order to maintain communication.

If you have heard of connecting via Bluetooth or Wi-Fi, you heard of wireless connection.

Most new electronic devices with communication capabilities built today have Bluetooth and Wi-Fi capability.

How Bluetooth works:

Bluetooth connects via radio waves. If you have a smartphone, most likely, your phone has Bluetooth capabilities. In many devices, the user has to switch-On the Bluetooth in the device in order to receive or send information.

I recommend that you always keep your Bluetooth OFF. Turn it on only when you really need it.

How to protect your Bluetooth enabled device?

According to *vectorsecurity.com*, 3.5 billion Bluetooth connected devices were shipped in 2017. It is found in almost every electronic device available today, from printers to phones, to the vehicles we drive, to electronic devices in our own homes.

When Bluetooth is activated, hackers have the capability to spread malware that might go completely unnoticed by users. No-a-days, unhealthy internet navigators have figured out how to inject cyber viruses via Bluetooth that can multiply or spread via Bluetooth. If you do not need to use Bluetooth, **keep it off**.

According to researchers at *Armis Labs*, "BlueBorne", a cyber attack via air, can affect almost any devices operating on Android, Windows, Linux, and iOS software before version 10. This means almost every computer, mobile device, smart appliance or other IoT[5] device running on the aforementioned operating systems could be hacked.

How Can You Prevent BlueBorne?

1-Update all software and passwords.
2-Turn Bluetooth services off when they're not in use.
3-Avoid public Wi-Fi networks.
4-Consider a virtual protected network (VPN).

If you find it necessary, consult with a trusted CyberSecurity provider to properly equip your device (s).

If you ever notice that you are not receiving expected calls or your phone battery drains faster than usual, check your Bluetooth connectivity. If it is on, TURN IT OFF, take the battery out, let it cool if it is hot or warm. Then, charge it again using a regular power adapter. It might improve the situation. But if it does not, take your phone to a professional able to identify the problem with your phone.

---

[5] Internet of Things, extension of Internet connectivity into physical devices and everyday objects.

WI-FI Connectivity:

Wi-Fi it is simply a marketing word that actually represents IEEE 802.11. Some people believe that Wi-Fi means "Wireless Fidelity." It does not. IEEE stands for *Institute of Electrical and Electronics Engineers*. *802.11* is standard for defining communication over a **wireless** LAN (WLAN).

802.11 (with no letter suffix) was the original standard in this family. 802.11 had to evolve due to original limitations. In each stage or standard, also known as *amendments*, a new suffix letter was added. According to *lifewire.com*, there are 24 amendments of 802.11. The latest 802.11 is 802.11y (Contention Based Protocol for interference avoidance). If you are interested in going deeper into this subject, visit: http://grouper.ieee.org/groups/802/11/Reports/802.11_Timelines.htm

Wi-Fi is present in many public places. If you are a traveler, you might have noticed the availability of wi-fi connection at airport waiting areas, restaurants, private clubs, and hotels. These physical areas of public internet access are also known as "Hotspots". Also, most mobile phone carriers offer plans that include private Hot-Spots connectivity.

Avoiding the use of public hotspots is highly recommended. The lack of encryption on public hotspots channels may leave your private information exposed.

Cyber Notaries, please, never ever use a Public hotspot to conduct cyber notarial sessions.

PUBLIC HOTSPOTS VS PRIVATE HOTSPOTS

Public Hotspots: are places with access to the internet where **everyone** with wi-fi enabled devices are able to connect to the internet.
Some places require agreeing with the service or inputting a dedicated password provided by the place itself. Example of public hotspots that require a dedicated password in order to access the internet are: hotels and restaurants. Although is a password protected accessibility, the connection still remains public. A third party has control over who has access to it or not.

Private Hotspots: are usually used by **one person only**. The private or portable hotspot owner has the ability to upgrade the encryption, change the network name, create complicated passwords, and, most of all, control who can connect to the hotspot. Be aware of the following: when enabling the private hotspot from a portable device such as mobile phone, the network provider for that particular mobile device's account might charge the bill with "Data used." Read the specifications of your portable device Network provider.

CARE FOR THE ENVIRONMENT AND DEVICES

There are, at least, 3 types of environments that you, the user, want to make sure are well maintained:
the intangible environment of your electronic devices where the software dwells in, the ambiance where you keep your devices, and the environment of your mind.

1-Intangible Environment:

Whether your electronic devices are the latest in the market or a few years old, it is recommended that the software running the devices is updated every time an updated version is available. Think of it this way, when your devices let you know that a new update is available, most likely, there are new threats out there that your software or App needs to recognize in order to keep your devices safe. Also, it might have to do with compatibility with internet browsers and/or the actual software/ App running internally in your electronic device. In software world, updates happen constantly. Keep an eye on them and maintain software/apps updated with the latest version available. It will not only protect what you do when connecting to cyberspace, but it will also keep your connection running properly.

Another area of the Intangible Environment of your electronic devices is the capacity and power your electronic devices count on. Develop the habit of checking memory space, defragmenting your computer from time to time in order to free

24

up trapped unused space in the system, and checking installed applications. If there are applications that you are not really using and the electronic device does not need them either, delete them. You want to keep your electronic devices running the software that you really use or need. It is about keeping the intangible environment of your electronic devices as healthy as possible.

2-The ambiance where you keep your electronic devices:

Make sure to keep your electronic devices in dry/cool places, out of reach of pets, children, and anyone who may tamper with the devices.
Keep your devices clean and charged.

Although there are several general accessories that work with your devices, do your best to use the ones that came with your devices or are the same brand.

3- **The environment of your mind:**

Keep a vigilant mind set and train your mind to recognize unusual activity observed when operating your electronic devices. Train yourself not to panic nor get emotionally unstable when noticing that the unexpected happened and you do not know how to fix it. Example: Apps quitting unexpectedly.

Education is key in keeping your mind aware of unusual activity in your devices. Education enhances your cyber awareness and the way you respond to situations that involves cyber-environments.

Note: Any instability in any of the 3 types of intangible environments could impact the safety of transactions or operations conducted in the cyber-environment.

The RISKS of ((Public)) Hotspots

Protect your electronic devices

Turn Wi-Fi and Bluetooth OFF when not in use.

➤ How can anyone be safe in the current cyber-environment where many minds from all traits have access to Cyberspace? The answer is not focused on those minds, but in you, your mind, and your user habits.

➤ A **cautious user** is someone navigating cyberspace, intentionally, avoiding potential problems.

➤ Keeping updated the software your computer runs in order to access the internet is another highly important step to take and repeat as many times as needed.

➤ Where there is a vulnerability, most likely, there will be a hacker trying to exploit it. You, as the user, want to counter anything that could make your cyber-navigation vulnerable.

➤ Many electronic devices have the capacity to connect via bluetooth and wi-fi (IEEE 802.11).

➤ Wired transmission, usually, uses traditional copper telephone lines already installed to homes and businesses.

➤ A better wired connectivity is run via **fiber optics**; a technology that converts electrical signals to light pulses (on/off) and sends the light pulses through transparent glass fibers about the diameter of a human hair.

➤ Five ways to secure your wired connectivity:
1-Auditing and Mapping.
2-Network update.
3-MAC Address filtering.
4-Use Virtual Private Networks (VPN).
5-Physically, secure the Network.

➤ Wireless connectivity does not require a cable in order to transmit or receive communication.

➤ If you have heard of connecting via Bluetooth or
wi-fi, you heard of wireless connection.

➤ Bluetooth connects via radio waves.

➤ Best way to protect the Bluetooth capability of your electronic device is by keeping the Bluetooth OFF. Turn it ON only when needed.

➤ "BlueBorne", a cyber attack via air, can affect almost any devices operating on Android, Windows, Linux, and iOS software before version 10.

➤ How to prevent "Blueborne" on your electronic devices that have not been updated to Windows 10:
1-Update all software and passwords.
2-Turn Bluetooth services off when they're not in use.
3-Avoid public Wi-Fi networks.
4-Consider a virtual protected network (VPN).
5-Consult a cyber specialist if you do not seem to figure it out.

➤ Wi-Fi it is simply a marketing word that actually represents IEEE 802.11.

➤ IEEE stands for *Institute of Electrical and Electronics Engineers.*

➤ Public Hotspots are places with access to the internet where everyone with wi-fi enabled devices are able to connect to the internet.

➤ Private Hotspots are usually used by one person only. The private or portable hotspot owner has the ability to upgrade the encryption, change the network name, create complicated passwords, and, most of all, control who can connect to the hotspot.

➤ There are, at least, 3 types of environments that you, the user, want to make sure are well maintained:
the intangible environment of your electronic devices where the software dwells in, the ambiance where you keep your devices, and the environment of your mind.

FROM A CYBER NOTARY TO CYBER NOTARIES

When you are online with a customer, remember that you are also a cyber-public officer with the ability to counter fraud. Developing the skills needed to the point that they become embedded into your online notarial services will enhance your focus when online.

You might be saying to yourself: "I already do enough as a Notary. Why do I have to add more to my responsibilities?" Well, when it comes to conducting Remote/Online notarizations, there is an add-on to your role as Notary Public; the role of a Cyber-Agent, Think about the following: most likely, at the beginning of your commission, you were just a Traditional Notary, or what I call TN. Then, you may have had the opportunity to develop skills in order to become a Mobile Notary, or what I call MN. Then, you may have entered in what it is known as Electronic Notary, or what I call EN. Finally, your State or Commonwealth probably approved Remote Online Notarization, and you are in the process of becoming a Remote Notary, or what I call Cyber Notary or CN. Each type of Notary requires certain skills. Having the capacity to provide services as TN, MN, EN, and CN does add to the ways you are able to get documents notarized, reach out to people, customers reaching out to you, and your notarial business counting with more options in order to increase revenue.

More than anything I have mentioned in the previous paragraph, one of the most exciting aspects of becoming a certified online Notarization Specialist is witnessing the transition to a new Era in the notarial field. Traditional notarial work will continue to be prestigious and admired by all notaries who understand the essence of what we do as notaries; however, it seems that when it comes to transitional times in societies, what the system in place offers is not what people want but what the system needs in order to cover what we have today and keep the vision open to future generations. Right now, the system that might move society to the direction needed in order to get things done, improve, experience progress, etc, is the ability to legally conduct Remote Online Notarizations.

What we are experiencing now in the notarial field was already predicted the day the first computer network was created. How do I know this? Since the invention of computer technology, societies with access to such technology has only developed more opportunities within the computational field. Technology is getting faster, more powerful, and smaller in size. It is saving thousands of dollars if not millions to businesses, including small business in the notarial field. The ability to conduct Remote Online Notarization saves commissioned notaries a lot of money and keep the notary public safer. Prepared and educated Remote Notaries save energy, fuel, money while maintaining higher levels of physical safety. No matter who the online customer is, the online customer will not be able to harm in any physical way the Cyber Notary.

Today, we still count with experts in the Traditional Notarial field who passionately offer their services and educate other notaries as well. A Cyber notary needs the passion and knowledge of Traditional notaries in order to render excellent notarial services online.

If as a traditional notary you have learned and developed the habit to place your Notarial Seal in a way that will not block any wording and place it where it is supposed to be ; next or by your Notary Signature (At least in the Commonwealth of Virginia it is that way), your Cyber Notary abilities will follow through with the same dedication placing the Digital Notarial Seal in such a way that it will not block any wording of the document or Notarial Certificate.

Being a Certified Cyber Notary , or what I call CCN, adds tools and skills to your professional notarial services. Generations today, young and old are finding out they do not need to leave home or office in order to get a document notarized.

In regards to mastering The Code of Cyber Awareness as a CN, I recommend becoming a CCN. Education is key to the awakening of your Cyber Awareness as Online Notarization Specialist or Cyber Notary. Your Cyber Awareness and how you implement that awareness is the Key to The Code to a safer Cyber-Environment when conducting Remote Online Notarizations.

If you have not yet, and you are able to legally conduct Remote Online Notarizations from the State or Commonwealth that commissioned you, become certified as Cyber Notary as soon as possible. Go to: https://www.CNVTA.club

CYBER NOTARY
VIRTUAL TRAINING ACADEMY

TRAINING CYBER NOTARIES TODAY

PII CONSCIOUS PROTECTING CYBERSPACE

Once you have received your Certification as Online Notarization Specialist or Cyber Notary, gather the necessary equipment, dedicate one device for your Remote Notarization Services, and protect yourself and your business by obtaining a Cyber Insurance. Remember, we deal with Personal Identifiable Information (PII). Just like you probably protect yourself with an Errors & Omissions Insurance, do the same with your notarial online services. Get a Cyber Insurance once you set up your Notary Business.

Need more information on Cyber-Insurance? Contact GetCyberInsurance@gmail.com

CH 3 REVIEW

➤ When you are online with a customer, remember that you are also a cyber-public officer with the ability to counter fraud.

➤ When it comes to conducting Remote/Online notarizations, there is an add-on to your role as Notary Public; the role of a Cyber-Agent.

➤ Having the capacity to provide services as TN, MN, EN, and CN does add to the ways you are able to get documents notarized, reach out to people, customers reaching out to you, and your notarial business counting with more options in order to increase revenue.

➤ Notaries today are witnessing the transition to a new Era in the notarial field.

➤ When it comes to transitional times in societies, what the system in place offers is not what people want but what the system needs in order to cover what we have today and keep the vision open to future generations.

➤ The ability to conduct Remote Online Notarization saves commissioned notaries a lot of money and keep the notary public safer.

➤ Today, we still count with experts in the Traditional Notarial field who passionately offer their services and educate other notaries as well. A Cyber notary needs the passion and knowledge of Traditional notaries in order to render excellent notarial services online.

➤ Your Cyber Awareness and how you implement that awareness is the Key to The Code to a safer Cyber-Environment when conducting Remote Online Notarizations.

➤ If you have not yet, and you are able to legally conduct Remote Online Notarizations from the State or Commonwealth that commissioned you, become certified as Cyber Notary as soon as possible.
   Go to: https://www.CNVTA.club

CYBER-CRIME STORIES

Before navigating cyber-crime stories, I will give you a quick overview of cyber-crime history.

In the 1960's, the word "hacking" was associated with 'fixing'. The malicious association with hacking became evident in the 1970s when early computerized phone systems became a target. Technologically savvy individuals, called "phreakers" discovered the correct codes and tones that would result in free long distance service. They impersonated operators, dug through *Bell* Telephone company garbage to find secret information, and performed countless experiments on early telephone hardware in order to learn how to exploit the system. Previously, I mentioned: "Where there is a vulnerability, someone will try to exploit it." It was true then and it is true now.

The following may sound strange to you, but just like a person could be kidnapped, information shared on the internet could be taken away as well and a sum of money or some kind of trade could be asked for its release back to the owner. Entities such as Hospitals, school districts, state and local governments, law enforcement agencies, small businesses, and large businesses are just a few of the impacted ones by **Ransomware**, an insidious type of malware that encrypts, or locks, valuable digital files and demands a ransom to release them. This is how Ransomware works: the malicious software gains access to files or systems and blocks user access to those files or systems. Then, all files, or even entire devices, are held hostage using encryption until the victim pays a ransom in exchange for a decryption key. The key allows the user to access the files or systems encrypted by the program.

According to *digitalguardian.com*, in 2017, 1,783 ransomware complaints cost victims over $2.3 million. (This is one of the reasons why I recommend getting a Cyber Insurance. If you need one or want one, contact GetCyberInsurance@gmail.com

According to FBI.gov: Long before cyber crime was acknowledged to be a significant criminal and national security threat, the FBI supported the establishment of a forward-looking organization to proactively address the issue. Called the National Cyber-Forensics & Training Alliance (NCFTA), this organization—created in 1997 and based in Pittsburgh—has become an international model for bringing together law enforcement, private industry, and academia to build and share resources, strategic information, and threat intelligence to identify and stop emerging cyber threats and mitigate existing ones.

Also, the United States Air Force counts with one of the most advanced anti-cyber threats organizations that ever existed; CyberCom. In a way, you nor anyone needs to panic or stop conducting business in Cyberspace. You just need to minimize the cyber vulnerabilities that might be present in your current environment. Some of the good practices are:

>Backing up every vital file and system is one of the strongest defenses against ransomware.

>Software creators usually include regular updates that include patches to make software more secure against attacks. If you have a team in your business, designate one person to monitor the updates. The less people involved in the updates, the better. Sometimes, too many hands in the pot, spoils the soup.

>Add rules that clearly speak of what can and cannot be done in the company's computers.

>Most importantly, train your people. An untrained employee or simply not knowing who to implement good practices could be the greatest insider threat and create the greatest vulnerability to cyber attacks. Train yourself and the people you work with or who works for you.

Once again, protect your cyber-environment.
>Keep Your Firewall Turned On.
>Install or Update Your Antivirus Software.
>Install or Update Your Antispyware Technology.
>Keep Your Operating System Up to Date.
>Be Careful What You Download.
>Turn Off Your Computer.

More vocabulary before the Cyber Crime stories begin. This way, you can make sense of the stories.

CryptoWall: an advanced piece of malware, a variant of CryptoLocker.

CryptoLocker: a Trojan horse that infects your computer and then searches for files to encrypt.

Cyber Crime Story 1

The same week Thanksgiving is celebrated, a mom's laptop got hit by a ransomware attack. 5,726 files got locked by CryptoWall. The mom did not want to lose her files so she contacts the attacker through the ransomware's communication feature. The mom receives a reply: "pay to get the files back or lose them forever." The files were important to the mom, so the mom decides to pay. The attacker asks for $500 the first week and $1000 for the second week. If money was not received on the second week, files would be deleted forever. The mom not only had to come up with the money, but also had to learn how to transfer amounts in Bitcoins. (If you have never dealt with Bitcoins, at first will look a bit complicated). The mom eventually learns how to handle amounts in Bitcoins and pays. The mom ended up paying $1000 in Bitcoins. She was lucky to get the key to unlock her files after submitting payment.

It is NOT recommended to pay for Ransomware. It is better to report the Cyber Crime.

Another word you want to be familiar with is: **phishing.** This form of cyber crime is one of the most common. Phishing is the fraudulent practice of sending emails purporting to be from reputable companies in order to induce individuals to reveal personal information, such as passwords and credit card numbers. Phishing has evolved and can fool users if users are not paying careful attention to emails before opening them or clicking on the links embedded in electronic communication.

According to techinsurance.com, "Phishing evolved into sending automated campaigns to thousands, if not millions, of people to steal their credentials."

One way to avoid phishing in the workplace is by requiring a comprehensive security policy across the entire organization with strict governance. Having a system in place to quickly report any suspicious activity and taking immediate action will mitigate serious damage to your business. If you are a business owner, remember to have a Cyber Insurance in place as well.

More than emails, phishing has spread beyond the inbox to mobile apps, social media, and instant messaging platforms replicating exactly the apps we trust with sensitive data. According to Techinsurance.com: " Security technology is evolving to detect phishing, but threat actors are always adapting."

DSM.net informs that, currently, there are 8 types of popular phishing attempts: account notification, file sharing, package delivery, fake invoices, tax fraud, charity/donations scams, blackmail, and event-specific attacks.

Cyber Crime Story 2

In the past, many cyber impersonators targeted credentials in order to steal users information for banking or credit cards purposes. Now, impersonators are targeting your SaaS[6] services like *G-Suite* and *Dropbox*. These Cyber criminals want your business files or files.

There have been cases where files containing hundreds of emails have been hacked and impersonators have embedded themselves into those emails. Once hackers have access to one account, they can easily embed themselves and use it to send malicious emails to others in the company, expanding their access. The way they probably did it was by sending a message claiming that there was a suspicious login to your account or that your password expired, providing a link to a spoofed page. DO NOT FALL FOR IT. If you receive an email like that, call the company directly or visit the official website and log-in from there.

How to protect yourself or your company? Forbes.com recommends "turning on multi-factor authentication across your organization, across all accounts. This is now considered the absolute minimum you can do to ensure security online."

Keeping the cyber environment safe starts with you, the education you receive, and what you do with that education.

---

[6] A method of software delivery and licensing in which software is accessed online via a subscription, rather than bought and installed on individual computers.

Before getting into the next Cyber Crime story, let us, let me tell you about the Cloud[7]. According to Azure.microsoft.com, *The cloud is a metaphor for a global network of remote servers that operates as a single ecosystem, commonly associated with the Internet.*

In order to keep data in the Cloud secured, systemsandsoftware.com proposed the following: *To keep data secure, the front line of defense for any cloud system is* **encryption**. *Encryption methods utilize complex algorithms to conceal cloud-protected information.*

Have you heard the phrase "Money moves people"? Well, many cyber crimes are money related. Cloudpro.co.uk reported that the reason for cloud infrastructure to increasingly draw the eye of cyber criminals is that *cyber criminals are looking for alternative ways to generate income. due to reduction on ransomware and crypto-hacking attacks.*

Despite cloud attacks attempts, it seems that cloud computing is safer than local storage due to the fact that cloud computing counts with highly trained technicians. On the other hand, Users storing data in local devices might lack the sophisticated training or knowledge needed to properly encrypt data during the storing process.

One breach could cost a company thousands if not millions of dollars. Merging to Cloud computing seems like a smart step to take. Be prepared to understand the thought pattern behind the cloud computing structure and how it functions.

---

[7] *Cloud* computing means storing and accessing data and programs over the Internet instead of your computer's hard drive (pcmag.com).

Cyber Crime Story 3

In July 2018, ft.com published a cyber crime story that conveyed the impact of "Red Apollo", a Chinese hacking group who launched one of the largest cyber espionage campaigns. Several countries around the globe were aimed by this cyber crime where the hacking group targeted cloud services providers instead of companies directly. The idea behind the attack was to spread spying tools to a variety of companies around the Globe. The cyber attack was known as Operation Cloud Hoper. According to Cyber Security experts, the Hoper attack did not cause serious damage to the targeted list; however, it had costly and damaging implications.

The complete story is found at https://www.ft.com/content/4f990a78-537a-11e8-84f4-43d65af59d43

Cloud computing is great. Remember, the cloud is connectivity over the internet and the ability to store and have access to your files over the internet instead of your tangible computer. Example of a cloud environment is: your saved documents in Google Drive. You can open your Google drives documents from any computer that has access to the internet.

CH 4 REVIEW

➤ In the 1960's, the word "Hacking" was associated with 'fixing'.

➤ in the 1970s ,when early computerized phone systems became a target, technologically savvy individuals, called "phreakers",discovered the correct codes and tones that would result in free long distance service. So the word "Hacking" adopted a negative connotation by the malicious perception it received.

➤ **Ransomware**, an insidious type of malware that encrypts, or locks, valuable digital files and demands a ransom to release them.

➤ You need to minimize the cyber vulnerabilities that might be present in your current environment.

➤ The National Cyber-Forensics & Training Alliance (NCFTA), became an international model for bringing together law enforcement, private industry, and academia to build and share resources, strategic information, and threat intelligence to identify and stop emerging cyber threats and mitigate existing ones.

➤ **CryptoWall:** an advanced piece of malware, a variant of CryptoLocker.

➤**CryptoLocker:** a Trojan horse that infects your computer and then searches for files to encrypt.

➤**Phishing** is the fraudulent practice of sending emails purporting to be from reputable companies in order to induce individuals to reveal personal information, such as passwords and credit card numbers.

➤Keeping the cyber environment safe starts with you, the education you receive, and what you do with that education.

➤One breach could cost a company thousands if not millions of dollars.

➤The front line of defense for any cloud system is **encryption**.

➤Encryption methods utilize complex algorithms to conceal cloud-protected information.

➤Despite cloud attacks attempts, it seems that cloud computing is safer than local storage due to the fact that cloud computing counts with highly trained technicians.

➤The cloud is simply the connectivity over the internet and the ability to store and have access to your files over the internet instead of your tangible electronic devices.

CHAPTER 5

THE CODE

The previous chapters were a warm up. I hope that by now you have an idea what The Code to a safer cyber environment is. If not, I am confident that this chapter will clear up the clouds in your head and help you focus on what you need to see in order to recognize and accept the responsibility that brings knowing The Code.

I have traveled to many countries. No matter where I was, the code was the same. The code transcends cultural barriers, language, and even spiritual beliefs.

Now, Cyberspace is an environment that embraces its own language; ones and zeros, the binary language. The ones and zeros may be camouflaged by what I call: Computational Dialects; Linux, OS, Windows, Python, CC+ or any other programmable Cyber environment. No matter what shape it takes, behind all algorithms, there is a pulse sending a valid signal (one) or invalid signal (zero) and the combination of both. The universe within cyberspace floats in binary codes. Are there any empty spaces? Probably not. If anything, maybe there could be inactive spaces in Cyberspace codified with a bunch of zeros without ones.

Now , to get you closer to the understanding of The Code, a few environments will be put into perspective: Home or personal, office or business, public, and International.

THE CODE AT HOME

No matter where you live, the safety of cyberspace navigation at your home or private space depends on you, the user. Even if you are not Information Technology inclined, as Cyber User, you have a great responsibility the moment your fingers, your voice, or your eyes command the software installed in your computer to gain access to the internet.

When computers reach your house or private space, they depend on you, not the other way around. Now-a-days, a computer could be a laptop, desktop, your mobile phone, your smart watch, or a smart toy. Anything that has internet access capability depends on you, not the other way around. The user is the commander of any operation. Therefore, cyber navigations depend on the Commander's cyber awareness and steps taken during the cyber navigation.

Reflect on the following:

<>How many times have you left the room while your computer is on?

<>How many times have you left the web-camera on while network access is also on?

<>How many times have you used your mobile phone while conducting internet business at home?

<>How many times have you forgotten to turn the Antivirus on before accessing the internet?

<>When was the last time your personal computers had an update?

<>Are you the only person using your computer at home or private space?

Is your home network a protected network?

<>When you navigate the internet at home, what websites do you go to?

<>Do you click links you do not know what they are about?

<>Do you click links because they have attractive words or images?

<>Do you open emails from unknown senders?

<>Do you save private identifiable information in your home computer?

<>Do you know how to encrypt files?

<>Do you know how to send encrypted emails?

<>Do you invest time in educating others at home about internet access?

<>From 1 to 10, how cyber ready do you believe you are?

<>When was the last time you read an article about current news in cyberspace?

<>Are all the applications (apps) you use in all your electronic devices updated with the latest version?

It may sound like a lot; however, once a natural routine, it becomes the minimum standards in your cyber home environment. If you run a business from home, be zealous about protecting your home-business cyber-environment.

If you are a family person with children, or visitors who tend to gravitate toward the electronics available at home, to include video game consoles, set rules, educate children and visitors on cyber awareness. Pass on The Code of Cyber Awareness to anyone who utilizes the equipment connected to the cyber environment in your home. It is ok to initiate a conversation about cyber awareness. Be preventive and proactive when it comes to protecting your cyber environment at home or private space.

The Code is You and in you, the one with authority to do something about preventing cyber vulnerabilities.

OFFICE/ BUSINESS ENVIRONMENT

The business environment is an interesting place. Usually, everyone has a job description linked to a pay rate. Most of the focus goes to the job description, which is perfectly ok. However, today, most companies are linked to an Internet network. Even if your job has nothing to do with Information Technology but you still use a computer or any device connected to the internet at work, you, as the User, have a responsibility. The Code also applies to you even if you are not getting paid for it. Educated Cyber awareness is the responsibility of every User with access to a grid or the internet. Developing good cyber habits at work will serve as preventive mechanism. The last thing you want at work or any place with access to the internet is to be the one who caused the development of a cyber vulnerability. According to research, hackers are constantly looking for vulnerabilities in all types of cyber systems.

If your work environment does not have a preventive plan in order to deter cyber intrusion, talk to your boss or Executive Officer. At executive levels, there are steps to take in order to keep a company safe from cyber attacks, or at least, have responsive resources when a breach occurs. If you discover that the company you work for does not have Cyber Insurance, contact GetCyberInsurance@gmail.com

If you are the highest seat or sit among those who make executive decisions, propose and support Cyber Awareness education.

If you are not even close to those who make executive decisions at the place you work at but know that a Cyber Awareness plan needs to be put in place, let them know. While they figure things out, activate The Code of cyber awareness in the area your job takes place.

If and when your job description allows it, reflect on the following:

<>How many people have access to the same electronic equipment/computers?

<>Is anyone downloading information from external links into the office computers? It could be pictures, music, videos, etc.

<>Are you able to educate those around you about Cyber awareness?

<>Do people in your work environment know the difference between Surface Web, Deep Web, and Dark Web?

<>Have you heard anyone talking about visiting the Dark Web from work?
<>Have you noticed people plugging in their phones or other devices into the computers at work?

You might not be getting paid to educate others around you about Cyber awareness. However, if no-one else is doing it, someone must. Protecting the Cyber environment at the workplace is everyone's responsibility.

Many times, people bring bad cyber habits from home to the workplace. Sometimes, they are unaware of their bad cyber habits. Hackers count with the lack of educated information in environments that could lead to opportunities that will benefit the Hackers.

The Code indicates that Cyber Education must take place when situations like the one above exist.

Think of every possible scenario at work that could lead to a cyber breach. Then, take The Code in you and begin to counter any possible way your office could be protected from any cyber attack. If you decide that it is not your job to brainstorm about cyber situations at work, then, contact the person who monitors cyber activities and find out if your area of work is well informed and cyber secured.

When it comes to the Cyberworld, everyone is involved in preventing cyber attacks or in opening a vulnerable link to the next hacker in line.

I hope that by now you know that The Code is the Cyber awareness in you and what you do with that information.

PUBLIC PLACES

Public places are one of the most vulnerable cyber environments. Public wi-fi is open to anyone with access to the internet from his/her electronic device. Encryption, usually, is not present in public networks. To Hackers, public networks are a mine of all kind of information traveling from one point to another. Not only private information could be exposed, but also malware could be lingering waiting for the next User to plug-in a USB cable that connects to an electronic device.

Public places are tricky. I tell my Online Notaries Colleagues: "Don't ever conduct an online notarization from a public Network infrastructure. Let your customers know that you need time to get to a private or more secured Internet Network. Customers will understand and appreciate it."

The Code that drives the Cyber awareness in you reminds you to apply caution. If you are going to check your Facebook page from a Hotel's Internet network, know that what you do on that internet network might be exposed.

Another common and well utilized public place is the Airport. Travelers tend to plug-in their electronic devices into Charging-Stations available at airports. Plugging-in the power cord might be safer than plugging in a USB cable to any of the USB sources available at airports.

When traveling, if Bluetooth is not needed, turn it off. Walking around airports with the blue-tooth on might make your electronic device vulnerable to sophisticated malware shared over Bluetooth. Blueborne is transmitted to electronic devices by air via Bluetooth. Please, keep the Bluetooth off as much as possible when traveling.

Recently, I had to travel to a Conference in St. Louis, Missouri. The travel itinerary had me stopping at a couple of Airports before reaching the final destination. The battery of my mobile phone was low and I had already used the portable charger. I had to find a power outlet in order to get the power bar on my phone green again. Intentionally, I had to look at every charging station available. Most were packed with laptops and cellphones plugged into the available power sources. I observed how a person unplugged a device and another person came in and plugged-in a new device using a USB cable. It was done naturally, no second thought, cables in and out. The apps on my phone were up to date, but I did not want to expose the software of my phone to any potential threat already in the air or those USB connections. I made sure the Bluetooth of my phone was Off. Eventually, I ended up turning the phone completely off. The phone had a thin red line of power. I saved it. Thankfully, I did not have to make a call and there was enough to keep myself distracted instead of navigating my phone or the internet on my phone. *Hudson News* had enough books and magazines to keep me busy.

Other popular public places are *Starbucks*, *McDonalds*, pizza places, and businesses that want your business/money. Be mindful of the vulnerability those public networks present. Notice that the "Free Wi-Fi" advertised and available on those places does not say:
"free encrypted wi-fi or free secured wi-fi".

Public places might be fun, but it also present a plethora of cyber vulnerabilities.

Use The Code; keep your cyber awareness activated.

INTERNATIONAL

We live in a Global society now. However, the word "International" still represents the connectivity among Nations.
Whenever you travel to a Nation that is not your home country, other rules might exist in regards to internet navigation. Respect the rules and keep your electronic devices safe as well.
If your home country is The United States of America, you might be aware of the constant Cyber attacks that try to penetrate the USA's Cyberspace. I am not here to say who is doing what or where and when the cyber attacks began. However, as a citizen or resident of the United States of America, and also as a possible business owner, putting into practice the qualities of

a **cautious user** when traveling overseas or within countries in the American Continent will add a layer of Cyber protection. If the electronic devices you travel with are linked to any network in the USA, a door is there to be open. Keep The Code of Cyber awareness active, the firewalls on, bluetooth off, and if possible, obtain a temporary electronic device that you can use when traveling to other countries. You do not want your electronic devices to become a channel that hackers may use to conduct cyber attacks against the USA.

It sounds like a lot to be aware of. It is not once it becomes natural to you and embedded into your personal Cyber Awareness Code.

The Code = You+ Your Cyber education + You as Cautious User.
The Code = You+ Cyber Awareness.

➤The code transcends cultural barriers, language, and even spiritual beliefs.

➤Cyberspace is an environment that embraces its own language; ones and zeros, the binary language.

➤No matter where you live, the safety of cyberspace navigation at your home or private space depends on you, the user.

➤The user is the commander of any operation. Therefore, cyber navigations depend on the Commander's cyber awareness and steps taken during the cyber navigation.

➤**When running** a business from home, be zealous about protecting your home-business cyber-environment.

➤The Code is You and in you, the one with authority to do something about preventing cyber vulnerabilities.

➤**At work away from home:** Even if your job has nothing to do with Information Technology but you still use a computer or any device connected to the internet at work, you, as the User, have a responsibility; to minimize cyber-vulnerabilities.

➤Hackers count with the lack of educated information in environments that could lead to opportunities that will benefit the Hackers. In other words, ignorance is a powerful tool to hackers.

➤Public places are one of the most vulnerable cyber environments.

➤**Blueborne** is transmitted to electronic devices by air via Bluetooth. (Keep Bluetooth off when not in use).

➤When traveling to a Nation that is not your home country, other rules might exist in regards to internet navigation. Respect the rules and keep your electronic devices safe as well.

➤**The Code** = **You+ putting into practice Cyber Awareness.**

SUMMARY

Chapter one gave you an overview of what Cyberspace is about. It lightly touched the differences between the Dark Web, Deep Web, and Dark Internet. From the aforementioned, the Dark Web is the one you do not want to get involved with during your internet navigation, unless you are a CyberCop and you belong to that special group of educated people able to track cyber criminals. This chapter also mentioned the Surface web; here is where the indexed web pages are found via Google or other popular search engines. When web pages that are legal are not indexed and not found via popular search engines, most likely the information is kept in the Dark Internet. Remember, **"Dark Internet" and 'Dark Web' are considered different.** In the Dark Internet scientific or similar data is found. In the Dark Web, illicit transactions occur. **Dark Internet is the same as Deep Web. The Dark Web can be found within the Deep Web. Dark Internet is huge. The Dark Web is only a piece of it.** The Dark Web is the "black sheep" of the whole Dark Internet.

Chapter two unveiled the qualities of a **cautious user;** the one who navigates cyberspace, intentionally, avoiding potential problems. This chapter mentioned the importance of software maintenance, wired and wireless connectivity, and how to protect the connection.

Chapter three directed words to Commissioned notaries asking them to embrace the transition to a new Era in the notarial field. The words in this chapter would probably make sense to public notaries and people who understand what notaries go through when developing skills as Public Officers.

Chapter four shared Cyber Crime stories and definitions Users should be aware of in the Cyberfield. Cyber Crime is real and evolving.

Chapter five clarifies what **The Code is all about; you + your ability to put into practice cyber-awareness.** It also provides the use of The Code at Home or personal, office or business, public, and International. To all video gamers, keep The Code activated when playing online games. Friendly information shared with other games around the globe could be used by sophisticated cyber criminals. **CyberVideoGamers, please, do not share personal information when playing online games.**

The Cyber World is in constant evolution. Artificial Intelligence is on the rise, cyber users continue to adapt to what it is available at the time of their cyber engagement.

Each generation might experience a new phase of Cyberspace. Whichever phase you happen to experience, keep The Code of Cyber-Awareness active. It will always be your choice to enter the cyberworld and navigate as a Cautious User. Enjoy the Cyber-Era you find yourself in.

CYBER-VOCABULARY

- ❖ ALGORITHM: unambiguous specification of how to solve problems.
- ❖ ANDROID: mobile operating system developed by Google.
- ❖ APP: a software application that can run through a web browser or offline on your computer, and on a smartphone phone, tablet or other electronic devices, including smart TVs and smartwatches.
- ❖ ARTIFICIAL INTELLIGENCE: the theory and development of computer systems able to perform tasks that normally require human intelligence, such as visual perception, speech recognition, decision-making, and translation between languages.
- ❖ AWARE: having knowledge or perception of a situation or fact.
- ❖ BINARY: in computing, calculations using ones and zeros.
- ❖ BITCOINS:: digital currency in which a record of transactions is maintained and new units of currency are generated by the computational solution of mathematical problems, and which operates independently of a central bank.
- ❖ BLOCKCHAIN: a system in which a record of transactions made in bitcoin or another cryptocurrency are maintained across several computers that are linked in a peer-to-peer network.
- ❖ BLUEBORNE: combination of vulnerabilities capable of being spread by air via outdated bluetooth..
- ❖ BLUETOOTH: short-range wireless interconnection of mobile phones, computers, and other electronic devices.
- ❖ BROWSER: a program with a graphical user interface for displaying HTML files, used to navigate the World Wide Web.
- ❖ CAUTIOUS USER: a person who navigates the internet in a preventive manner in order to protect the cyber environment and, at the same time, avoid vulnerabilities from developing.
- ❖ CCN: Certified Cyber Notary.
- ❖ CNVTA: Cyber Notary Virtual Training Academy.
- ❖ CLOUD: in computing, it is a network of remote servers hosted on the Internet to store, manage, and process data.

❖ CODE: In computing, it is a set of instructions. In Awareness, it is the combined knowledge and perception of specific situations.

❖ COMPUTER: an electronic device for storing and processing data, typically in binary form, according to instructions given to it in a variable program.

❖ CRYPTOCURRENCY: a digital currency in which encryption techniques are used to regulate the generation of units of currency and verify the transfer of funds, operating independently of a central bank.

❖ CRYPTOLOCKER: it is a malware, a trojan horse that infects the computer and then searches for files to encrypt.

❖ CRYPTOWALL: a form of ransomware. **Trojan horse that encrypts files on the compromised computer. It then asks the user to pay to have the files decrypted.**

❖ CYBER: relating to or characteristic of the culture of computers, information technology, and virtual reality.

❖ CYBERAGENT: in this case, it is a person conducting business on cyberspace. Example: Cyber Notary.

❖ CYBERATTACK: an attempt by hackers to damage or destroy a computer network or system.

❖ CYBERCOM: United States Cyber Command (USCYBERCOM) is one of ten unified commands of the United States' Department of Defense. It unifies the direction of cyberspace operations, strengthens DoD cyberspace capabilities, and integrates and bolsters DoD's cyber expertise.

❖ CYBERCRIME: criminal activities carried out by means of computers or the Internet.

❖ CYBEREDUCATION: Education online.

❖ CYBERENVIRONMENT: See Cyberspace.

❖ CYBERFILES: files stored on the Cloud.

❖ CYBERFIX: a problem solved on cyberspace by the use of cybertools or cyber thinking.

❖ CYBER-INSURANCE: insurance product used to protect businesses and individual users from Internet-based risks, and more generally from risks relating to information technology infrastructure and activities.

❖ CYBERKNIGHT: made up character by the author of this book. Imagine a Cyber Agent with an Armor on.

❖ CYBERNOTARY: Commissioned Notary Public who conducts Remote/Webcam Notarizations via Internet.

❖ CYBERSECURITY: the practice of defending computers, servers, mobile devices, electronic systems, networks, and data from malicious attacks.

❖ CYBER SOCIAL MEDIA: social media in cyberspace. Example: Facebook, Instagram, Pinterest, Twitter, LinkedIn, and so on.

- ❖ **CYBERSPACE:** from a mind set, it is a notion of an intangible world. It is also an electronic medium used to form a global computer network to facilitate online communication.
- ❖ **CYBERVIGILANT:** active cyber-awareness.
- ❖ **CYBERVULNERABILITY:** flaw in a cyber system that can leave it open to attack.
- ❖ **DATA:** in the computer world, the quantities, characters, or symbols on which operations are performed by a computer, being stored and transmitted in the form of electrical signals and recorded on magnetic, optical, or mechanical recording media.
- ❖ **DARK INTERNET:** the overall internet that lies under the Surface Web. It is not indexed and not found through popular browsers. Good and bad is in this dark cyberspace.
- ❖ **DARK WEB:** the black sheep of the Dark cyberspace. Illegal operations occur here. Dark Web is found within the Deep Web.
- ❖ **DEEP WEB:** is unindexed data beneath the Surface Web.
- ❖ **DIGITAL DEVICE:** A physical unit of equipment that contains a computer or microcontroller.
- ❖ **DIGITAL VIDEO:** is an electronic representation of moving visual images (video) in the form of encoded digital data.
- ❖ **DROPBOX:** personal cloud storage service (sometimes referred to as an online backup service) that is frequently used for file sharing and collaboration.
- ❖ **DSL:** digital subscriber line which is defined as the way a computer connects to the Internet at high speeds using telephone lines.
- ❖ **ECOSYSTEM:** system of interdependent components that enable cloud services. In cloud computing, the ecosystem consists of hardware and software as well as cloud customers, cloud engineers, consultants, integrators and partners.
- ❖ **ELECTRONIC DEVICE:** components for controlling the flow of electrical currents for the purpose of information processing and system control.
- ❖ **ENCRYPTION:** the process of converting information or data into a code, especially to prevent unauthorized access.
- ❖ **FIBER OPTICS:** A technology that uses glass (or plastic) threads (fibers) to transmit data.
- ❖ **FIRMWARE:** permanent software programmed into a read-only memory.
- ❖ **FLASH:** short for *Adobe Flash*. It allows Web developers to incorporate animations and interactive content into their websites.

- ❖ **FLASH DRIVE:** a small electronic device containing flash memory that is used for storing data or transferring it to or from a computer, digital camera, etc.
- ❖ **G-SUITE:** comprises Gmail, Hangouts, Calendar, and Google+ for communication; Drive for storage; Docs, Sheets, Slides, Forms, and Sites for collaboration; and, depending on the plan, an Admin panel and Vault for managing users and the services.
- ❖ **GUI:** Graphical User Interface.
- ❖ **HACKER:** a person who uses computers to gain unauthorized access to data.
- ❖ **HOTSPOTS:** wireless LAN (local area network) node that provides Internet connection and virtual private network (VPN) access from a given location.
- ❖ **HTML:** Hypertext Markup Language, a standardized system for tagging text files to achieve font, color, graphic, and hyperlink effects on World Wide Web pages.
- ❖ **IEEE:** Institute of Electrical and Electronics Engineers.
- ❖ **INTERNET:** a global computer network providing a variety of information and communication facilities, consisting of interconnected networks using standardized communication protocols.
- ❖ **iOS:** an operating system used for mobile devices manufactured by Apple Inc.
- ❖ **iPHONE:** a smartphone made by Apple that combines a computer, iPod, digital camera and cellular phone into one device with a touchscreen interface.
- ❖ **JAVA:** programming language that produces software for multiple platforms.
- ❖ **LINUX:** an open-source operating system modelled on UNIX.
- ❖ **MALWARE:** software that is specifically designed to disrupt, damage, or gain unauthorized access to a computer system.
- ❖ **MAC ADDRESS FILTERING:** a security access control method whereby the MAC address assigned to each network card is used to determine access to the network.
- ❖ **NCFTA:** The National Cyber-Forensics and Training Alliance.
- ❖ **NETWORK:** A computer network is a group of computer systems and other computing hardware devices that are linked together through communication channels to facilitate communication and resource-sharing among a wide range of users.
- ❖ **OPERATING SYSTEM:** the software that supports a computer's basic functions, such as scheduling tasks, executing applications, and controlling peripherals.
- ❖ **PASSWORD:** a string of characters used for authenticating a user on a computer system.

- ❖ **PHISHING:** fraudulent practice of sending emails purporting to be from reputable companies in order to induce individuals to reveal personal information, such as passwords and credit card numbers.
- ❖ **PII:** Personal Identifiable Information
- ❖ **PYTHON:** an interpreted, high-level, general-purpose programming language.
- ❖ **RANSOMWARE:** a type of malicious software designed to block access to a computer system until a sum of money is paid.
- ❖ **REMOTE WORK:** This one may also be known as telecommuting when a person, instead of working from a central office, works from a place with access to the internet. Today, there are many businesses without central offices making the work 100% remote.
- ❖ **REMOTE NOTARIZATION:** the legal act of conducting notarizations, live, via web-camera over the internet.
- ❖ **SECURED URL:** Uniform Resource Locator. It is the address of a World Wide Web page or file on the internet.
- ❖ **SOFTWARE:** the programs and other operating information used by a computer.
- ❖ **SPYWARE:** is software that is installed on a computing device without the end user's knowledge. It enables a user to obtain covert information about another's computer activities by transmitting data covertly from their hard drive.
- ❖ **SURFACE WEB:** also called the Visible Web, Indexed Web, Indexable Web or Lightnet, it is the portion of the World Wide Web that is readily available to the general public and searchable with standard web search engines.
- ❖ **UNIX:** Powerful, multi-user, multitasking, and extremely stable 32-bit computer operating system and the platform on which the internet was built and continues to work. Written in C language, Unix comes with built-in TCP/IP protocols and can run on practically all types of computers from mainframes to desktops and handheld computers.
- ❖ **URL:** Uniform Resource Locator. It is the address of a website or file on the internet.
- ❖ **USER:** person operating the computer.
- ❖ **VPN:** Virtual Private Network.
- ❖ **VIRTUAL:** not physically existing as such but made by software to appear to do so.
- ❖ **VIRUS:** malicious software that, when executed, replicates itself by modifying other computer programs and inserting its own code.
- ❖ **WEBSITE:** a location connected to the Internet that maintains one or more pages on the World Wide Web.

- ❖ WI-FI: wireless networking technology that uses radio waves to provide wireless high-speed Internet and network connections.
- ❖ WIRED: connected using cables. Most wired networks use Ethernet cables to transfer data between connected PCs. In a small wired network, a single router may be used to connect all the computers.
- ❖ WIRELESS: connected without cables.
- ❖ WLAN: wireless LAN, is a network that allows devices to connect and communicate wirelessly.

SOURCES

https://www.lifewire.com
https://www.google.com
https://www.symantec.com
https://usa.kaspersky.com
https://www.yourdictionary.com
https://searchitchannel.techtarget.com
https://www.nature.com
https://www.webopedia.com
https://searchmobilecomputing.techtarget.com
https://www.techopedia.com
https://techterms.com
https://searchsecurity.techtarget.com
https://www.businessdictionary.com
https://en.wikipedia.org
https://www.cnvta.club
https://digitalguardian.com
https://FBI.gov
https://www.techinsurance.com
https://Azure.microsoft.com
https://www.globussoft.com
https://www.vectorsecurity.com

www.ingramcontent.com/pod-product-compliance
Lightning Source LLC
Chambersburg PA
CBHW021019180526
45163CB00005B/2029